AF526701

Beyond Earth and Sky!

WRITTEN BY MANNAT
COVER BY RIDDHI PANCHAL

Copyright © Mannat Gupta 2021. All Rights Reserved. No part of this publication may be reproduced or transmitted in any form or by any means, mechanical or electronic, including photocopying and recording, or by any information storage and retrieval system, without permission in writing from the publisher. Requests for permission or further information on usage the of this document should be addressed to: contactmanokay@gmail.com

Legal Notice - The Purchaser or Reader of this publication assumes responsibility for the use of these materials and information. Adherence to all applicable laws and regulations, federal, state, and local, or any other jurisdiction is the sole responsibility of the Purchaser or Reader. The Author and Publisher assume no responsibility or liability whatsoever on the behalf of any Purchaser or Reader of these materials.

ANY PERCEIVED SLIGHTS OF SPECIFIC PEOPLE OR ORGANIZATIONS ARE UNINTENTIONAL

The one who has seen
the darkness can see the light.

Dedicated to all my readers

Preface

Dear friend,

Some words when arranged together by heart and soul are not only true to the core but so potent that they carry the strength to energize your spirit or perhaps make you weep, happy, ecstatic, and quenched, and take you to a place never traveled before, completely unknown and rewarding.
I'm glad to say that poetry is not dead like palpable letters; it is still alive and lingering in every one of us, wanting to lose, take an expression, or melt.

In my opinion, poetry could be used as a tool to go into the unknown and complete what is left unfinished or experience what you never had. Moreover, I feel it is never meant to be studied but only experienced as art is something that cannot be examined to dissect what benefits it entails. It can only be understood in subliminal or metaphysical ways or through expression.

If you do music, paint, play, dance, write, sing, compose, make people laugh and happy, or simply live for love, with love, you are an incredible artist.

Never stop!

I believe we all are artists painting our lives incessantly and we all have the potential to achieve whatever we aspire to cultivate. P.S. I hope you have a good time and great life!

Much love,
Mannat

POEMS

Chapters

Chapter 1 - Love

Pensive heart
And strong walls
Will melt soon
When comet falls
Bell jars will horn
Mysteries
And
The Moon will sing
A beautiful hymn
When you reach within

Strengthen the strings
Of autumn and spring
Eternity and time
Approach the sun
And boldly become one.

Love is not abstract
It can be physical too
Like we are tangible
And intangible through.
Love will always rule
Both kingdoms
Of heaven and hell
A road not defined
But journey instead.
A beautiful flower
Too can smell,
Lose its charm and spell
But always has a story to tell
And power to make bees dwell.

- An empty page

An empty page
Like
An empty heart
Wants to pour love
And profound art.
Sometimes no meaning
Just life
Unknowable
Unknown
And
Unified

Love is not simple
Or confounding
Its incandescent fire
May burn your body
To reach
Your core
Help you to
Know more and more.

And

Become one
Indestructible
Infinite
In love

The hopeless romantic

A thread is holding me
And holding you,
Unfolding me
And folding too.

Embracing me
And what is true.
It wasn't easy
When it was new.

With persistence
I have learned to use
Power of stillness
Is my muse.

I can hear
You and me
And me and you
Love is intangible more
And tangible few.

I don't want you to come
Until I heal and learn,
Be more gentle and kind.
Great love is what I want to find.

When you find yourself truly, you are full
and overflowing, not missing or needing
anyone. You are home. If somebody comes,
it's beautiful, if you are alone, it is beautiful
too. Then find love or perhaps it will find
you. The love which cannot be known by
just the mind but every inch of you. Where
you love like a lover not needy.

-- unknown

The years I have spent
Without you
Are now coming to an end.
Everyday,
Voices in my heart say
You are coming to stay
And will never go away.

I'm cold
Writing letters in bold
To hot my pen
And cool my pain.

I miss the tree
Tall, dark, and green
That once belonged to me
Now I do not see
Recollecting
The intimacy!

Love is rare
Not everyone know
Neither they touch
Nor they show.
What people call love
Is just unknown.

Your intimidating eyes
Never despise
Yet surprise
With depth
They seek
And push me to speak
Express my heart
With no dearth.

It is a drug
I must not fall
Two people in love
Against all
Savoring winters
Warmth of balls
Dancing secretly
Around the hall
If love is true
And above all
Why do we hide
And call it off?

To your
Beautiful, palatable eyes
Intimidating too
Full of muse
But only to me
As I seek
Beauty of no time
Holding a strain divine
Dear eyes of my
Valentine!

He was in no haste
And I couldn't hurry
The solemn twine
Unnecessary

Hearts hiding
Across the vine,
Gossamer and blurry
To the naked eye
But not earth and sky.

When you say
You want me to stay
And I am your home,
Without me
You feel so alone.
The soul inside my heart
That cannot be seen
By human eyes so keen
Can be felt
So strong
As my heart melts.

I try to write you,
Paint you,
Sing you,
And compose you
In sync
With my beating
Pensive heart,
Trying to soft
What is hard.

Love cannot be explained
Fools try to write
Flowers make bees dwell
Lovers love to show
It is the peculiar feeling
When butterflies
do not go away.
Eyes feel quenched
Comprehend even French
Cheeks undergo mild fatigue
Mind bears stillness
When heart throbs
Lips get subliminally moist
Hands and feet clench
Beginning a new end

Your eyes
Are like a book
With never-ending pages
I'm trying to read
I feel the need
To complete
The chapter
we left behind
To find it
In this lifetime.

I embody you
You embody me
What our souls are
Only we can see.
We were split into two
To be the world's muse.
We have no other option
But to always choose
As we had a pact
Before we came back.
Dare to divine
What heart lacks.

True and complete
Show all what we feel.
Teach every soul to find
The power of mind.
When two souls in love merge,
They can never diverge.
Love is pristine
Be it alone or in a team.

I am still to go into depths
With each of my deep breaths
Know love
Show love
Sow love

Why do you come
Only at night
When it is dark
And bright inside?

Chapter 2 - Fearless

I can hide
Let no one know
I feel good
Only sometimes I show
Terrify me
The thought of the day
When I could no longer say
No complacence I want
Or love of certain amount.
You shall see my account
When I am no more around.

My most coveted pen I set,
For the love
I am yet to get...

-A writer

For those who do not know
The power of her
I urge you to observe.
Help her embrace
Remind her she is brave.

- To all the men and women

I'm writing this letter
Which I'm never gonna find
In the hope of getting better
And focus on my mind
I just can't comprehend
This feeling
There is something I don't know
I'm burning
But I'm cool
Not cool
But trying to be

Unable to concentrate
Incomprehensible mental state,
Fighting my dark thoughts
Not letting them penetrate
What is this feeling?
Why it isn't revealing?
What does it want?
What is my fault?
Why are you locking
me up in the vault?

Open the door
I want to see more
And roar
Like never before.

One thing I have learned:
Not to concern
Or berate myself
For not being the one
Who is always
Perfect and flawless
Without
Imperfections and cautious.

It's okay to have flaws
Not always work for applause
Accept and move ahead
Try to connect
Learn the dialect.
Select what you want
Kill the questions that haunt
Let him or her flaunt
You are beautiful and strong.

Some days are not good
That doesn't mean,
You could
Let yourself down
For just one fault found.

'Tis time for my tree
To be free,
To nourish
Till the beautiful
Flowers flourish
And everyone
Becomes enchanted
With my energy
And Flowers scented.

If you doubt your potential
You must know
It's essential

Some things are beyond your
Comprehension
And your name is mentioned
In the most prominent section
Of the book
You know in fractions

You are yet to complete
The Transaction
Addition and subtraction.

I need a goodbye
From all the people who deny
My existence or happiness
Give me a feeling of emptiness.
Goodbye with no sigh
I cut all the ties
Of you and I.

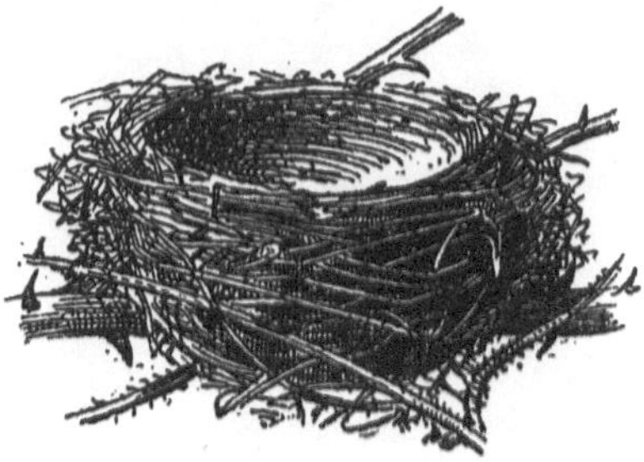

Unwanted rest
Nests of distress
Beneath the shroud
Turns around
When lines are crossed
Victories are loud!

I wonder where the time goes
Sun rises and trees grow
Moon shines and stars glow
Mouth opens and eyes roll
Love betrays and hate grows
Heart shrinks and soul matures.

My brain is no more mine
Neither this body
Of flesh and wine,
I lost it
Now I can't find
Sense gratification
Made me blind.
I succumbed
To my lower self
And I need your help
I am ringing the bells
Join me again
I will bear the pain
Do good to change
Break the chains

Today, I did no bad
But still I'm not glad
My heart feels stabbed
Lips are chapped
Nose is runny
Even when the day is sunny
I loved her with all my heart
Even when the world
Tried to tear us apart.
The voices in my head
I will never forget
The pain you gave me
Now you shall never see
My sympathy, compassion, or love
But I forgive you
Hate flies away with the Dove!

Hearts are ductile,
They melt with a true smile.
Collect the memories
And then unwind and see,
Enjoy the ecstasy
Of reminiscence
And images so serene,
Now perhaps a dream!

There is a rule I have made
Before I go to bed
I forgive everyone and
Count my blessings instead
Take 5 deep breaths
To clean my head
And move ahead.

I am no victim of my mind
Body and soul are mine
Depth I seek, to break the bind.
Truth, complete truth
And love in my bowl
Makes me gratified and whole.

When I was
The victim of my mind,
Couldn't see the power
It made me blind
Hide from the pain
And live in vain.

No more my mind could tame
Or bring
Somber, sorrow, or shame.
To overpower your mind
You have to stop to lament,
And teach your monster to be
Kind.

To make this world
A better place
It is your response_ability
To clean your space,
Be no victim of your mind
Leave it all behind.

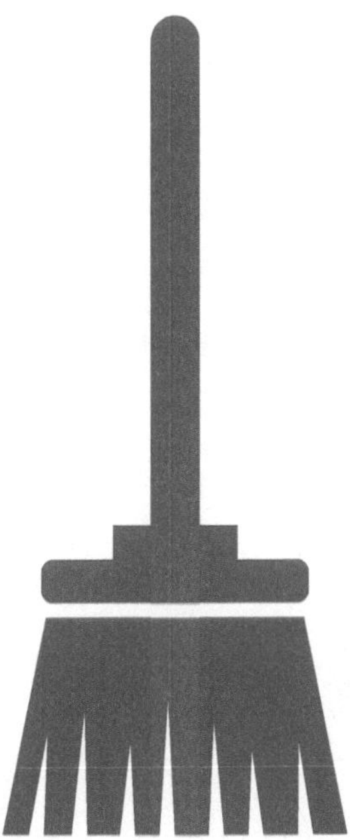

If you are struggling to find
What makes you spellbind
Close your eyes
Sit on the ground
Hear all the voices found
Let go
Do not fight
When you see some unwanted Sight
Or hear any fear
Practice, practice, practice
Until you make it clear
One day you will find
What makes you spellbind.

When I was little
Perhaps four
My father told me
About the door
Where people get lost
In the hope of getting more.
The mystery may lure
But you must be sure
Before you go inside
And see sights to endure
Beyond that door.

Dear Heart,
They might call you a
Fledgling,
Sliding unlike a swing.
But if you stop,
They might cut your wings
Run! Run!
Sorrow must not come.

Whenever pain, sorrow,
Or hopeless
You feel,
Sit on the ground
Or walk on the grass to heal.

Remember

Your tired, exhausted,
Flabbergasted
Self
Needs your utmost care
And immediate help.

To all the immortal souls
Seeking to fulfill
Thy glorious goal
Must not stop
Impediments are meant to cross
Thy path to glory
Thy mesmerizing story
Death mustn't scare you
It shall come only to dare you!

When I am down
I just drown
In the ground
With sorrow
And let the river
Flow

Can't stop
When I recall,
Then I
Take my pen
Make it dance
See the beauty
Give it a chance

To empower
And glance
At what I have penned
Helps me comprehend
And defend
Who I am.

When I look in the mirror I see
Handsome trees and me
Inspiration to seek
They cannot speak
Yet they glow
Look beautiful
Even the willow.
Dry leaves too make fashion
Sometimes they go on vacation.

How do you define
the beautiful vine?

Dry, naked, tall wood,
Pink flowers looking good
or
Green, juicy, Chandan tree
Branch full of fruits and
Snake-free.

Beauty is both
Front and hind,
Hard to define
But not to find.

Chapter 3 - The Sky

The sky
Which seems to be so high
Is the highest
Holds even the heaviest
Planets, Sun, Moon, Galaxies,
Even the universities
Of never-ending Universe.
Trying to converse
The most sophisticated
Beautiful rhythm
Which can be found within

Some things
Are yet to be found
Perhaps
The mysteries of sound

I want to bring unknown
To this known world
Solve all the coils curled
Travel to galaxies of
Never-ending universe
Find the answers I urge
As I go deep and deep
Only one thing I seek,
The body which is mine
For sometime
Where all the
Answers are lying
Is the most profound book
Asking me to open
My eyes and look.

Part of me is part of you
Little did I know
When it was new
The seeds we sow
In the ground
Become alive
When love is found
We all are one
Even the sun
Together we elevate
Alone we separate
We are souls
Who complete the whole
Yet we alone are complete
There is no need to compete.

Water is precious and pristine
Turns brown into green
Blue to red
Put anxiety to rest

Not even a day could go quiet
Without touching water
And is more vital
When the days are hotter.

Some days
The tap
Tip-toes
Tip-toes
Tip toes
And drop by drop
It just flows
Burning unnoticeably slow

Some eyes do not see
Water makes us and trees.
I do not want my Grandchildren
To curse me
For leaving water expensive and
Less
Together we can save and
Express
Our gratitude to water
And once again make it fresh.

When I close my eyes
I am ready to go
Into the sky
To meet the bottomless sea
Into the sea
To meet the capacious sky
Both are one
But poles apart
I wonder
If they see each other or not.

I never thought of
the potential
Of my mind
To comprehend
The beauty of creation
Happiness has a new definition
Every cell, electron, proton
Dances in ecstasy
As mysteries unfold
In front of my eyes
Still naïve to discern
Countless lives.

Ocean, trees,
Cold and hot breeze,
Are responding for free.

Their love for us is
Unbiased
Un-polluted
Un-finite

Not all can see
Not all can feel
Not for everyone
It is real.

Music boils my blood
Until I can't stop thinking
And it teases my soul with
Cool ecstasy
Lying in the mind:
Dormant
And sometimes burn
With an incandescent
Expression of existence
Trapped Inside a cave
Wanting to lose
And melt.

The taste that you define
Of good food and love
Is perhaps the same
Like food pleasures the body
Love pleasures the soul
But flesh must die,
Love cannot,
One is immortal
The other is short.

Bluebirds are taking their leave
From sun, sky, and still trees.
Bees too are planning a vacation,
They have had enough radiation.
Now it's time to go
I count till
One, two, three, four!
Five no more.

Oh, clever man!
I call thee
Standing in the heart of a bee
Who's due has been unpaid
The nectar has been taken
Without freight
No more will thee
Get my love so kind
To revenge your glutton mind
Return or else pay
I'll come back
Is all I can say.

I'm no longer me
I lost myself
When I found the key
It was never a dream
Now I do not sleep

The day I died
My grave was found
To bury
What I borrowed
From the ground

- Close your eyes.
What do you see?

Is there any
beginning or end?

My universe is inside me
I can feel and see
Galaxies
Inundating me
With the knowledge I seek
Wanting me to speak
Let the world know
What my universe
Has to show
I have a message to glow
I am in everyone
And everyone is in me
If you solve the clue
You will be free.

I find a way to find me
The new journey excites me
Solar System
Full of wisdom
Man and Woman's kingdom
Full of mysteries
To overcome miseries
With unending history
Of slaves
Where women were raped

Men killed men
For victory and wealth
Cheated on their health
For pleasure, not peace
Is now to change
As together we un-arrange
Rules that are strange
Are coming to an end
New life will surge
As we merge

Pleasure with love
Love with Pleasure
Self with-in
Suffering will go
And hearts will sing!

The end
MOVIE

Calle de San Juan, 2
La Habana
Cuba.

A Letter

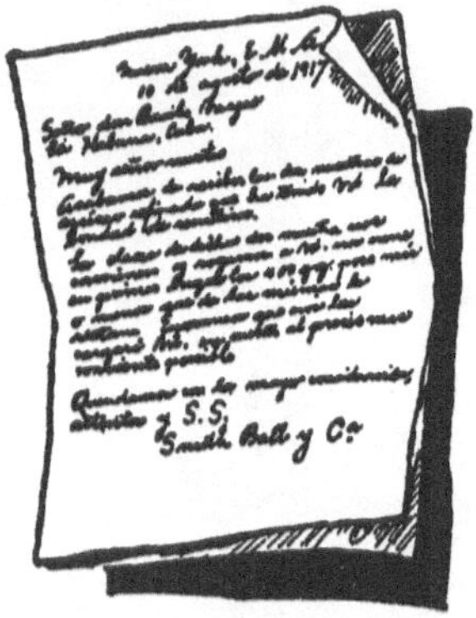

From the bottom of my heart, drowning in the sea of gratitude, I thank you for your presence. I hope you had a good time.

A year back, I was not quite certain, what I wanted to be, who I am. I took a break from traditional compulsive activities, focused within, spent my time in solitude and in intimacy with pen and paper, and I think I am never going back.
I consciously started writing poems late last year, without any intention of writing for anybody.

I never anticipated I'd be composing poems, and now after writing probably 100s of poems, it feels like I have been writing since the dawn of the earth.
I wrote incessantly listening to music, reading Emily Dickinson, Austen, Keats, Charlotte Bronte, and some of my friends too inspired me.

I'd like to extend my special thanks to Ian, who helped me edit the poems, Manay and Sujal for graphics and videos, Riddhi for the beautiful cover, Falguni for beautiful edits and assuring everything is perfect and in place.
If you like my poems or would like to know more about me, you can find me on Instagram or email me.

Instagram- beyond.earth.and.sky
Email - Contactmanokay@gmail.com

P.S. Your feedback/review can help me grow this book. Let me know if you have something to share, I'm so excited to hear from you!

Thank you,
Sincerely
Mannat

Great poetries cannot be explained, it has to be felt, and I am sure when you pick this book up, it will give you rush of emotions. Anything I write or say won't do justice to this book, there were many moments in the book where some lines connected straight to my heart. If you are someone who wants to handpick a poetry book, this should be the one.

Arjun Sachdeva
Book Influencer on Instagram and YouTube
Username: silly.reader

"Beyond earth and sky is a collection of short poetries. Powerful , Passionate and inspiring. "

Tanya Panda,
Book Influencer on Instagram
Username: baebookish

"Beyond Earth and Sky is a dreamy journal of thoughts written by a magical pen. The poems will allow you to appreciate everything around you and within you."

Falguni Jain,
Book Editor, and Influencer
Username: bookworm_falguni

"Work full of art! I'm Amazed.

Ridhhi Panchal,
Illustrator, Artist
Username: riddhiipanchal

www.ingramcontent.com/pod-product-compliance
Lightning Source LLC
Chambersburg PA
CBHW022147160726
48282CB00024B/208

* 9 7 8 9 3 9 1 2 3 7 4 8 6 *